The Cry of Oliver Hardy

# The Cry of
# Oliver Hardy

POEMS BY
MICHAEL HEFFERNAN

*Athens*
*The University of Georgia Press*

Copyright © 1979 by the University of Georgia Press
Athens 30602

Set in 10 on 12 point Monticello type
Printed in the United States of America

Library of Congress Cataloging in Publication Data

Heffernan, Michael.
  The cry of Oliver Hardy.
  I. Title.
PS3558.E413C7          811'.5'4          79–14599
ISBN 0–8203–0480–8
ISBN 0–8203–0485–9 pbk.

For Susan, Kathleen, and Joseph

# Acknowledgments

Thanks are due the publishers of the following periodicals and anthologies for permissions to reprint: "A Canticle of the Stars," from *The American Poetry Review*, © 1979, World Poetry, Inc.; "The Four Things" and "The Life of the Mind," © 1974 and 1977, *The Ark River Review;* "The Sore Subject," from *Barataria*, © 1977, The Barataria Press; "Saint Ambrose and the Bees" and "The Saint and the Lady," from *The Carleton Miscellany* (1979); "Daffodils," from *Carolina Quarterly* (1979); "A Quick One for Berryman," "At the Dark of the Year," "The Plight of the Old Apostle," "Fourth of July," and "Kennedy," © 1973, 1976, 1977, and 1978, *The Chowder Review;* "The Visitant," from *Counter/Measures* (1974); "Midwinter Sunday in Orion Township," from *Epoch*, © 1972, Cornell University; "In Blessed Weather," from *Heartland II: Poets of the Midwest*, © 1975, Northern Illinois University Press; "In Praise of It," © 1979, *Kansas Quarterly;* "Porsche," from *The Massachusetts Review*, © 1968, The Massachusetts Review, Inc.; "The Dream," from *Mikrokosmos* (1977); "The Table," "Rage Seated," "The Apparition," "A Figure of Plain Force," "How the Archangel Answered," and "February 1st," from *Poetry*, © 1969, 1972, 1973, and 1978, The Modern Poetry Association; "A Man of Parts" and "The Whereabouts," from *Poetry Northwest*, © 1975, the University of Washington; "Famous Last Words," from *Shaping: New Poems in Traditional Prosodies*, © 1978, Dryad Press; "Word from Under," © 1974, *Shenandoah;* "The Crazyman's Revival" (originally, in ten parts, "The Crazyman His Uproar His Fits & Starts"), from *The Shore Review*, © 1975, The Shore Press; and "The Rising," from *The Westerly Review*, © 1977, Split-Leaf Press.

"Nineteenth of April" was developed from: "Another Part of the Field," © 1977, *Shenandoah;* and "Nineteenth of April," in *The American Poetry Review*, © 1977, World Poetry, Inc.

"The Table" was reprinted in *The "Poetry" Anthology, 1912–1977* (Houghton Mifflin, 1978).

The author wishes to thank the National Endowment for the Arts for a fellowship grant which stimulated completion of this book.

# Contents

—It is impossible for us all to live the lives of hermits! exclaimed Mr Heffernan desperately.

Joyce, *Stephen Hero*

1

## The Table

To sit composing like a sunlit ghost
beside the window, saying: if the lost
wind quicken in the tree, the dancing heaven
thicken to snowy furrows by evening,
I will have less to tell you. Blue by green,
the lake is where three terns are drifting. When
a fourth, circling the air, settles beside them,
they tighten together on the wide surface.

Now they have lifted. All the window shows
is naked water and a green slope. Composing,
like the sun itself, making the light fall
neatly on each thing, is to mark the balance
within which we will find ourselves arranged,
oddly, in one room, at a stranger's table.

## Midwinter Sunday in Orion Township

She is outside trudging with the dogs.
The air is grayly brittle like the air
in Bruegel's *Hunters*. I am taking a bath.
When I think I have nothing to say,
I consider how many times

Balzac himself lay down,
perhaps not wrinkling his toes in a tub
but sprawling his broad self outward
to the soft edge of ease
listening for things to happen.

She is on her way in now. Their paws
and her boots are tapping
on the kitchen linoleum as she
tousles the snow from her hair
into blue and gleaming beads.

## The Dream

What sounded like rainfall kept up all night
into the early morning, so they stayed
a little while in bed until the light
gradually brightened from beneath the shade,
warming the sill and the few plants they kept,
and one of them was up to look outside
to see what it was doing while they slept,
and finding nothing he turned back inside
where she was sleeping, and the light grew dim
on the same sill that had been bright before,
as if the rain would come that troubled him
that night and make a sound against the door
much like the nightlong noise it made before
it woke him, against someone else's door.

## Porsche

Leaving it parked in one of Oxford's
medieval gullies, he took a bus to the outskirts
with shoppers and Kenyans
in the hands of a balding driver
who himself had trouble making change

      squat in a fragile back lane
      uneasy sunlight braising its hood
      and the tower of St Mary the Virgin's
      draped on the left front fender

He tilts top-heavy through factory suburbs,
wonders: where have they put Carfax Tower
the forehead-knocking pubs
and florid steeples, punts on the Cher

We will stop for bitters
round the next hedgerow
sign of the Lamb and Flag

      derelict, out of its element
      a regular thump gone from the back tires
      its grating whine quiet: slither of cloud
      in the finish, changing hue and form

One ruddy woman hugs at her groceries
like a fat child in her lap
seems she might tell them a story
and are well past Abingdon
will soon have a view

of the great Cathedral at Salisbury
am all but certain I've been here
left the key in the switch, the wipers
on, the ashtray smouldering

      altered now, clings to the
     flagstones, waiting storm, like a boat
     at anchor, and the streets, deserted, drift
     into windy shadow, St Mary's plump spire
     performs a miraculous hover

Would wrench that door, spin out into bushes
wave my thumb over my left shoulder
see if I'd get back by nightfall

      a thicket of flowering limestone
     the jungle itself in cooling daylight
     encroaches among lanes, among low doorways
     clutter of beasts and vine
     lifting it easily up by the chassis
     maps and tissues spilt to the floor
     dipping its nose in the gutter
     darkened, at mid-day,
     utterly laced-in, brambled
     forever, and forever abandoned

Have come to Southampton
Will book passage

## The Apparition

Trying to get the whiskey to do it and after that
lumbering out in the yard for a stray dog or a spook
shambling from nowhere: as you pause, consider the flat
gut of Orion, taut as a boxer's, how he took
some bobcat's hair off with his bare hands,
and for a time you're happy, having read that in no book.
Then you stroll back in like a man who demands
intensity, haul down the liquor for a last try,
and the kitchen's surly again like a crowd of urchins,
so you swagger to bed then, leave them alone
to dwindle behind you in the dry dark, while
whatever it is that whitens inside you, bone
or guardian angel, gathers up stair by stair
into the grisliest of apparitions,
staying your passage further into no more air.

## A Figure of Plain Force

You let the door sway open on its hinges
into a cleansing quiet where the sunlight
moves in the air like seawash among cool windows
and beyond them a stretch of open country
that strives into the sea. You have begun
nothing of consequence yet, though you may begin
by desperate measures something you left undone
or went to do and quit remembering.
In this condition you pretend to lean
solidly into the open while you gather
the winds about you by deliberate grace,
turning you into a figure of plain force,
careful and candid, never in a dither,
given to nothing noisome or unclean.

## The Rising

Tomorrow we will rise up off our beds
oddly bewildered, for the sumptuous
face of the tiger is inside the woods

and as he bends he bows and when he bows
the common day grows curious and then
he poses his great face in among the trees

like a broad moon rising. Once again
something is gorgeous in the atmosphere
as if some amiable thing had just been done

or of a sudden had grown comelier
and then the tiger dozes carefully
and all the light is like a frozen fire.

The last of birdsong is about to be
loosed from the stillness, and the air's repose
is chilly, so the next thing that we see

we shake ourselves loose and begin to rise.

## The Four Things

It was a morning in August when four things happened.
First a cat came into the room and lay down
on the edge of the floor and she was a cat
of even temper and clean habits and one of her habits
was to stroll in and stretch herself flat along the wall
arranging her prim face rigidly into her paws
until she was sleeping soundly. I knew if I moved
her eyes would glide up slowly and her toes spread open
and she would yawn broadly or begin to purr
so I deliberately did not move. A gust of wind
fell down through the flue like a great stone
plunging in water and ruffled the ashes up
which was the second thing. Then thirdly
the cat slipped away for no apparent reason
into another room and the door fell open
and a man said Good I see you are ready
I wish you would come now and the door flew shut
while the light in the room grew perfectly white and lonely
and outdoors as if from nowhere it had begun to snow.

## The Visitant

It was a moonless night the night he came.
The quiet fell about his ears in bunches.
Why he had come he had good reason for
but faintly understood the aimless game
he contemplated playing was pretentious.
Nevertheless, he scarcely felt the floor.

His lean face bore a bleak beleaguered look
like one of those old evangels on a portal
the rains diminish and the winds undo,
and yet he lingered in this lonesome nook
under the stairway for a shape to startle
the nimble whistler that should happen through.

Then lest a minute of the livelong night
transpire that he felt altogether safe in,
he wakened in himself a nemesis
fast on the verge of trembling into sight
or from behind to make his neck-hair stiffen,
till he grew wary, wanting out of this.

But nothing stumbled from another room
and nothing happened by and nothing happened.
Only an intimation of dismay
came squirming through him from that primal gloom
he'd blinked his lids on till the window opened
that spilt him headlong into the break of day.

Which is to say he dwelt within his own
authentic darkness and his knees were feeble,
though nothing worse than this had taken place—

nothing, at least, before the light that shone
faint as a firefly from beneath the table
rose and approached him with a grim grimace.

Appalled, he dawdled in a broad distress
that fell from nerve to nerve and made him founder,
and then the lath and plaster came undone
and the whole air was one unruliness,
while through the flindered space they thrust asunder
twelve shapes came treading towards him one by one.

The breath spun like an updraft up his throat,
but he did nothing, and the room felt hotter.
What kept him rigid as a driven staff
after the floorboards had begun to float
like seawrack drifting shoreward in the water
was an old boldness on his own behalf:

"I'm at the brink of something imbecile,
some fit by which all clarity's confounded
unless I quell whatever quirk this is
that loosens me and keeps me several—
which having done, I'll crouch as I'd intended
under the dark these makeshift images

flow back from to the void wherein they grew
like so much swamp-gas." And at this his body
was folded in a frozen cloak of light
so cold he felt his inmost bones turn blue.
And he was crashing at the walls already
before we paused to watch him, put to flight.

# A Quick One for Berryman

*Bury me in a hole, and give a cheer*

The book he lately made some said was thin,
or so some hinted—
which is what the man wanted:
he did it haltingly with no heft or precision.

Say the elements of style Use no adjectives whatsoever
Use only nouns and verbs Use nothing else at all.
I find this of injunctions the most formidable.
Lord should I give in or do I dive for cover?

Say we fall down among the daft and mighty dead:
how can we come to lay things in their dire places?
Say I am fraught with noises:
what could I render plainer, what do I drop unsaid?

Here is a matter mainly of disposition:
the dubious thing is that none, not even a saint,
will comprehend the manner of my complaint
or the quaint fervor of this contrition.

Maybe I'll undergo some late abstemiousness
when my top part falters
and I am driven to avoid the shelters
I took to in my distress.

May be my timely fall will not seem cumbersome:
I had an uncle once kept foul as a sty
who swung himself from a trestle as the noon train flew by,
so nothing was left of him.

I have a dread I'll drop off, daintily.

# Fourth of July

All afternoon we did nothing but read,
she in her book about Josiah Wedgwood,
I in a history of England during the Georges.
Outside it was hot so we stayed inside.

Then we got trapped and bored and it got late
and just about then a firetruck came down the street
and the dog was howling so we went chasing fires.
Four houses down a roof was burning and they put it out.

When we got home we decided to go for a ride
in the country in our old Olds and the air was good.
No one was out there but us and a couple cows.
On our way back we stopped at Mike's and sat in his yard.

Mike's wife got us tea and Mike had some sparklers to light
along with some bottle-rockets which we watched him shoot
out of a milkjug and I showed him Scorpio behind some trees.
Then the mosquitoes started and we got bit.

When we got home we found out we were tired.
There wasn't much point in staying up so we got in bed
and pulled the one sheet over us and gave each other a kiss.
Whatever else was wrong, it hadn't mattered.

## In Blessed Weather

The light comes into the house and a few flies
stagger from light to shadow and again to light
where chairs and a table sit and the Armstrong floor

is clusters of squares among rectangles
lifting up bits of light, and the pair of chairs
that were my uncle's who died of a wintry life

edge up to my grandmother's table
that no longer looks like the table where I sat
in front of her Sunday suppers because my wife

decided to strip it down to the bare wood
one Saturday in the fall. One of the chairs
is altogether in shadow and the other

has one of its back rungs brightened by sunshine
while nothing more than a narrow lance of light
aims under it over the darkling squares

and a cat whose hair is black and white
treads into the place I'm in,
oblivious of this light, not even knowing the sun

has been drawn down into its deeps
behind our air and circumstance and weather
or that I am sitting here being the bard

reminding this place and every one of you
that I know where I am and that I do

precisely what I do because I do it
because I am the poet

that saw the dog that fled through my neighbor's yard
an instant ago so fast I would have had to
disrupt my train of thought to have said so
exactly when he did so

and because the flies still tumble into the light from somewhere
and the table and chairs are still and the cat reclines
with both paws extended over an arm of a chair made of wicker

opening his face to yawn
onto the light that comes all the way from the sun
to his twenty-one whiskers and all his hairs and claws

on a sunporch seven miles inside Kansas
at the end of October
in blessed weather.

## Word from Under

You watch an old dog drowsing in the weather,
a dull dog doing absolutely nothing,
brown rubbish in a leafpile barely breathing
that evidently will incline to lie there
the rest of today and maybe all day tomorrow
letting her life drift emptily down to zero.

This probably chastens the soul, to commune with zero
as an abiding presence in the weather,
neither plus nor minus, and to renounce tomorrow
as a pronounced improvement upon nothing
beyond some blind propensity to lie there
stiffly beneath the air and to keep on breathing

if only because you happen to be breathing,
having acquired such intimacy with zero
and known the solitude of those that lie there
expecting little but the daily weather,
that every effort is a kind of nothing
done for the sake of lasting until tomorrow.

But she is alive today and not tomorrow
and yet displays an aimless way of breathing,
marking her place there like a lump of nothing
precisely in the middle of the round world's zero.
Jaybirds bicker above her, while the weather
bleakly reviles her: "How can you lie there

like any wreckage that would have to lie there
soiling the scenery well beyond tomorrow?

You will grow rotten with redundance." Whether
or not she listens, she persists in breathing
as if, because she has begun with zero
or something like it that is all but nothing,

she has discovered how to live on nothing
and grown good at it so that she can lie there
blank as the genius that invented Zero.
This is the lesson that she leaves: tomorrow
you will attempt to empty your life by breathing
everything out of you into whatever weather

the weather has taken shape as and conceive of nothing.
All you must do is lie there with your mind a zero
and begin the next tomorrow by not breathing.

## Rage Seated

The air you breathe is derelict.
Your mind worn thin,
desire's extravagance drawn spare,
you spin in an orbit of your own devising
within walls marred yellow, crying
to bird and human: I am he that
thunders, I am the sky, I am
desperation, I am Wednesday morning.

The glacier is moving south.
Taking the sun's glint westward
you will bless yourself grandly at your own
peril, and all in a sweat like rainfall
will surely set out for the woods, grow seedy.
A wonderful redemption is moving south.

2

## The Crazyman's Revival
### 1

Crazy with love he was he was unhappy
so much his craziness had turned him over
and she that was all he knew she was uneasy
and the dark was around her so it was dark
in the marches of his mind where he fled for cover
sat among reeds and waited till he got sleepy
and woke in his room at daybreak and went to work
to lose himself among persons that were busy—
they nickel and dimed him to death in that humdrum—
and the one who was all he thought, how she would sweeten
even his deep insides that he knew were rotten
though the dark was around her still and the same daydream
kept up in the back of his head where he was lost
and crazy as a crazy beast

## 2

The real world wasn't there it was hardly even
the real world that it looked as if he saw
but something improbable something half alive
outside him on the borders of his watching
that looked back at him from the interwoven
tops of the trees raised up against the light
itchy with legged things that crept and crawled
and dropped around him if the limbs were twitching
Could be he bristled like a bug with life
or like some toad that dwelt among the timber
slept underneath row beside row of lumber
slotted above his head for a good roof
nails kept together—he approved of nails
He kept his distance from the animals

*3*

To which I answer Since the wind was blowing
& outside where the elms were the very walls
had blossomed & because
no one was looking I got lost
along a footpath in among some trees
Beyond a fence two horses bowing
beautiful faces while a man in overalls
struck off over stubble as they tossed
& tore the grasses When I looked again
the blue in the ground ascended out of the green
toward the tall blue sky In the meantime
the grieving yellow was forage & I & the horses
safely together before anyone could come
pulled open holes in the ground with our sweet faces

*4*

Right then he was filled with fear or something like it
The dire abandonment that he had made
when he made good his riddance
riffled his lids with symptoms of disorder
and for a while his life was all collisions
Oh but the thing he felt was delicate
and deep within him something kept him glad
saved him at least from suicide or murder
It was the kind of woe that waxes fat
if a man so much as lend it this much room
In short it had his backing he supported it
he kept the best of him in short supply
so all he did was sit there and attempt to hum
scraps of a tune he felt uplifted by

*5*

And was uplifted and was bravely bent
on coming down for only the deepest reason
if someone told him what this reason was
Some things one does not do
some things one never does
some things are seldom done
even by God's chosen
This is selfevident
He could imagine how they'd spite him later
taking the floor against him one by one
I do what I and you what you
he'd sputter And I've done it some before
when you were none the wiser
At this they rise up and condemn him more

*6*

When it got specially bad he began to think
He thought about the sick dog by the road
he found one time and put a bullet in its head
He thought about the spot that bullet made
on the dog's brow, wonderfully round and pink
He thought about the things he knew for sure
how men were lonely and lived lonely lives
how even the sun was lonely and on fire
He thought about the cry of Oliver Hardy
how he would dance with dread and tweedle his derby
and send his clear soprano up from all his tonnage
whenever the deadly husband with the knives
the murderous sailor or their own relentless wives
were about to do him and his pal some permanent damage

## 7

Once when I was and a tiny little boy
two of my mother's girlfriends carried me at Christmas
off to see Santa Claus & as we crossed the street
the wind was blowing & the one that had my hand
said Close your eyes to keep the dust out
At which I shot back—as the one
that told it some years later
claimed in a letter—
It's better to look where I am going & not get run
over than keep the dust out—
I believe I must have said that, much as I'm inclined
to think she recollected only the searching wit
of a sparkling boy, & me but the microcosmos
of the grievous child I grew to by & by

*8*

So then he sat down and he wrote all this
first one way then another then he said
The hell with it this isn't any good
Why don't you walk outdoors? That might be nice
So he went walking out, and it got worse
When he was finished he came home and slept
had one dream then another then he stopped
got up, went to the window and of course
it came upon him after all this grief:
he sat down and he wrote: The problem is
you have forgotten how to say your prayers.
He knew it. He felt good. He came to life.
Back at the window night was moving in.
He watched the glass go black. He watched him grin.

*3*

## At the Dark of the Year

Here is my winter sermon: two birds
on two bedraggled branches. Nothing
could make me like them. I could

talk myself blue in the brains, reciting
pity's or misery's morningsong
the whole hagridden morning: they will

still look blameless in the guilty chill
enough to worry me in my bones. Get up
the guts, the fool things tell me,

to say to the people: Screw your
strength up, buckle your courage on.
Tell them it was birds that told you.

## A Man of Parts

Later this afternoon they are coming
to take the rest away. It is almost autumn,
    leaving me no more choice but to go on
effortlessly, though in somewhat better humor
    than last week when they came for the French horn
and the week before that the Louis Quinze settee
    along with the cuckoo-clock collection
I began in Basel that miserable autumn
    after mother was shipped home in a crate,
leaving me nothing that I could do. One o'clock:
    I remember writing them a letter
and mailing it from Milano before I left
    for Brindisi in the rain (no sign yet
of when they will be here) only to let them know
    they shouldn't expect me home for some time
on account of the rainy season. One o'clock:
    idleness I despise both in myself
and others. Then off across the Adriatic,
    pausing at Corfu in that blue harbor,
blue beneath bluer hills, dreaming about those hills,
    dreaming to disembark and disappear.
How long has it been since that? Dolphins diving by,
    rough water between Naxos and Paros,
bottles jostling behind the bar, though we were warm
    beside each other while our whiskies slid
back and forth on the table and the barman sulked
    with everyone else asleep. Persistant
things like this I can't get rid of this afternoon
    while they are on their way, to take away
the rest of the whole damned business if they want it

one last time. One o'clock. What would you like
of all these brittle portions of a man of parts
    breathing alone in a forsaken place?
I can scarcely remember what your face looked like,
    the two of us pitching over the sea
like a pair of schoolboys huddled against the chill.
    I often dream you are walking towards me
and I can't make out your face. After they took her,
    week after week, even with you, I dreamed
she had been sailing in her crate to look for me,
    but I was always gone. Even with you,
she kept on sailing. As soon as they have finished
    they will bring you this. Maybe the autumn
will come along sooner then. The rainy season.

*February 1st*


This is the month the Romans swept the doorways
with brooms made out of rushes bound together.
I am upstairs attempting to write a letter.
What I could say keeps hiding in one corner
among the rack and ruin in my head,
cobwebs and dust, sheets on the furniture,

ghostly and sad as pointless furniture
in houses where the walls have secret doorways
and lonesome little breezes at the heads
of stairways where the dear departed gather
to murmur through you as you round the corner
on your way down one night to read a letter

from a longlost lover. I could start this letter
by taking a look around at the furniture:
an uncle's favorite rocker in the corner.
He scribbled about some girl in one of his diaries:
"It makes me sad to think we'll be together
only in Heaven. Sadie hit my head

with her fist today. Poor Sadie. My poor head."
He got relieved of Sadie sometime later,
though he and the other never got together,
except in Heaven. Too much furniture,
too many walls and floors, windows and doorways.
Down the front stoop, the sidewalk; past the corner,

he lurks around the lamps to the next corner.
She meets him by the drugstore, tilts her head,

coaxes him with her eyes: "Here, back in the doorway,
I want you now." One time he wrote a letter,
left in his strongbox: "I could furnish your
rent, your utilities. We could be together

the Friday nights S. always gets together
for pinochle with her ladies around the corner."
Sad news a person learns from furniture.
There are some things we none of us can hide.
We are the dead already whose loveletters
sparkle the air each night between the doorways.

One day the kindly coroner stands in the doorway.
Together the family settles the furniture.
Some lawyer sends good word on his letterhead.

## Famous Last Words

Is it a question, then, of getting up
the will to move from one place to the next?
I'm undecided, largely, at the start,
as always, though I guess I'm apt to see
a good bit better once I've had a drink.
It's still too soon for that yet. I can wait.

Sometimes I have to laugh: the more you wait,
the more you end up wishing you could up
and have a look at what will happen next.
Where did it ever get you, from the start,
the time or two you said you'd wait and see,
when all you really wanted was to drink

it all in, all of it, in one long drink
that would relieve you of the need to wait
for the Right Moment? A man's time is up
too soon in this quick world. As for the next,
I think I have a theory: first you start
to notice how you can't move, think, or see,

and this alarms you, so you try to see
what a person has to do to get a drink
in this place. No one drinks here, so you wait
a long time trying to figure out what's up—
a very long time, well into the next
two or three thousand years, until you start

to feel more lonely than you were to start
with, and you stay this way forever. See,

I'm realistic. And I need a drink.
The will to move is only the will to wait
in different terms: moving is when you're up
and ready for whatever happens next;

waiting is what you do when you're the next
in line and several others got the start
on up ahead of you and you can see
their dust rise off them. If I had a drink
instead of breakfast, I could stand the wait.
They'd probably like to know what held me up.

Maybe they'll send a man up here to see
what keeps me waiting. Maybe he'll say I'm next.
Maybe he'd like a drink before we start.

## How the Archangel Answered

What you can say about
it, as over against the kinds
of phenomena you
may be imposed on to deal with,
so long as you will be
able to do so at that time,
scarcely matters, being
no doubt extraneous to your
endeavor under those
quietly urgent conditions.
Encouraged instead, though
not so fervidly as usual,
to breast resourcefully
toward one colossal objective
of which you should record
some few mild suspicions, even
though you will find it not
altogether unbeguiling,
you might yet discover
the function of supplications.
Whether your natural
tendency, however infirm,
to pursue the abstract
can sufficiently counter your
attendant tendency
to avoid the precarious
will wholly depend on
something unwarrantable which,
at all events just then,
may not submit to direction.

Lacking a "policy,"
therefore, on the assumptions of
    which to approach the void,
your next and fatal requisite
    will proffer itself, in
part, by a quaint reminiscence:
    is this where you repair
elsewhere, as to adjoining rooms,
    there to await what is
to be awaited, or should you
    begin now avidly
reciting your deeds to the air?
    This ought to occupy
no more than an instant, during
    which, nonetheless, certain
alternative measures can troop
    into view, but you will
firmly dismiss them as doubtless
    unworthy, or rather
will *sense* them dismissed as if by
    a grave yet splendidly
casual instinct within you.
    At this point little is
further accountable, the state
    of your mind being now
irrecoverably transformed,
    while the light by which you
should now make out, for example,
    your fingers against the
doorlock or your shadow edging

up from the woodwork is
strikingly denser than before.
The inconsequence of
what you would say about it, in
spite of your urge to pass
through with an exquisite gesture,
will now grow markedly
obvious, and so you will think
you are bending outward
into the light like the light's twin.

## Stubb Makes His Bed among Sun, Moon and Stars

Up in the heaven there were bright assassins
that plowed the deep with faces white as linen.
Somewhere inside me I fell into a sleep
where there were women moving from door to door
up and down an alley off a narrow street
where I had been walking all day like the ghost
of the stranger I used to be in those times.
Next thing I knew I was in with one of them
and I could see her breast looking out at me
from among her dresses that kept flying up
over her head like big sheets of heat-lightning
and then her belly was beckoning at me
and I was in my stockings beckoning back.
It was no use. In the orchard of the sky
I was grabbing for cherries, great ripe red ones.

## The Sore Subject

I was sore from the neck down. Even the ends
of my two lean elbows were sore and the hairs
which crowded up to my navel like a flock
of pilgrims that trekked all this way to see it
said Goddamn we don't feel so good, it must be
the altitude or something in the water
or maybe we're just exhausted from the trip
or maybe Jesus what in the hell was that
Let's get the hell out of here. As for my balls
believe me they were the sorest place of all.
It was as if the proverbial little bird
who comes around one time in a million years
had begun to peck me to bits by perching
on the tip of my penis where he could poke
that once-in-an-epoch dent in my poor balls
then lift away to wander back into Time
leaving them bruised and broken a million years.
But Oh I'll get along there, I said, reaching
to cup my right hand round them while my great friend
thickened serenely behind the ragged spot
where the bird's immemorial claws dug in.
I'll be okay there too, I sighed, abstracted.
But I was sore all over—in thumbs and toes,
thighs and ankles; the creases behind my knees
caused me intensive trouble from their drawn skin,
and each of the bumps on both of my nipples
had been ticklish hillocks of sorrow longer
than I could remember; my belly-ripples
were mottled and red from soreness deep inside,
and all except my head, as I have mentioned,

most of me down to the bottoms of my feet,
was one long age of soreness personified.
In the middle of my brains where the soul lived
were other birds that caroled in a green wood
so sweetly and unceasing that I could sleep
and sleep a million years if I needed to.

## The Whereabouts

Whenever he found himself there, whenever
he was at large and his whereabouts unknown,
with someone trying to find him—say, the wife
or the man from the credit-card company
or the cops—though he never did anything
and was never the kind of person that did;
whenever, in short, he was ever wanted
to make an appearance or come into view
for whatever reason, he was never there,
not ever in one place where you could find him.
In case you expected to notice the note
he left on the dinette in the breakfast nook
on his way out through the breezeway, look again:
there isn't even a warm place where he sat
with his forehead into his arms or the ring
where the shotglass was from which he steeled himself
against his departure, or so much as one
whiff of his cigarette or his after-shave,
because he didn't drink and he never smoked
and he thought men's toiletries were unmanly.
As for him crouched over with forehead in arms,
come now, he was hardly that type of person.
Whenever he found himself off to himself,
the question of where he was didn't matter,
no matter whether others were overwrought
or however many, from some blind concern,
pursued him, blindly, into his whereabouts.
Wherever he was, whenever he was there,
it wasn't special, what he did, believe me.
All he had to do was make his face go blank,

imagine his eyes and nose and mouth away,
until the whole front of whatever he showed
was a snowfield over which a snowfilled sky
leaned like a great blank lady down from heaven
for whom he had been waiting week after week
since the last time he remembered where he was.

## The Plight of the Old Apostle

It came to this, if it came to anything:
my brave ambition was adrift in heartache,
so that I winced and grumbled and tried to look
as if it unbecame my hard-won standing
as a higher form of life around this place,
but what it was that did this I could not tell,
though once or twice I got to the verge of it:
the thing hung in me in a great drape of steel
that boomed and rattled when I went to move,
like an onslaught of ugly weather that drove off
dogs and belongings and townsmen to high ground,
with a few loose papers tumbling the alleys,
a lost child lurching from corner to corner,
the churchbells chiming no one to services.
I stopped short of wondering where it would end
or for what reason I was suffering so—
I who had done no wrong in a life of toil
and whom the dread of ruin or sudden death
had never once bewildered with indolence.
What wore me down was not so much how to lift
this rusty stupor that was over my mind,
but how to get up alive in spite of it.
I nurtured a thousand possibilities.
The one I liked the best involved leaving town
and taking up residence in a small cave
above the harbor on a whitewashed island
where the girls were shy but willing and the life
was easy as picking figs off the figtrees
that clung to the hills against a spotless sky,
and the bartenders all grinned when you sat down

and woke you with a drink after siesta.
Now this was the life I knew I'd like to live,
and come to find out it was this life I was
heartsick about—a life in another life
I might have dreamt of once on waking: a sky
so blue you went all blue walking under it
and your face turned glassy blue when you looked up
and the girls said nothing and hardly had to
because they knew you and you knew they knew you
and said so by the way they nodded toward you
or half smiled from the balconies as you passed
beneath them, and one of them let down a grin
so wide you could step through it and disappear
into the teeming bramblebush of her skull—
a dark so dense you lost your bearings in it
and came out on the other side wise and blind
and able to prophesy and aim the sails
of men ambitious after things men desire
and only the dead have lost ambition for.

# The Life of the Mind

Then he looked up and said, The snow is falling:
deep snow will be here by nightfall; everywhere
snow on the lawns and in the crotches of elms,
long gray canyons of it where the cars go by,
and even though now the air is thick with it
about the treelimbs and the gabled rooftops,
tomorrow morning the same trees and houses
will look alone and foolish as if the snow,
which left them so, said: I was only falling;
I only fell because I needed to fall:
there was this greenness under me; I was white,
from miles in the air where only whiteness was,
so I decided I would lie around you,
fall out of pure joy or out of lack of joy
on every hollow and every crooked thing
that the world beneath me gave me to fall on,
easing my whiteness perfectly everywhere
till I was more than whiteness, I was the white
pronouncement of a world that resembled me.
And then he said, The snow is falling harder:
it would be better if I got up and left:
the air is thick with flakes the size of eggshells,
and only the leeward portions of the trees
resemble trees. If I should get up and leave,
perhaps I would be safe in another place;
perhaps some other place feels safer than here.
And then the snow said, from among the houses,
from limbs and rooftops and from all the spaces
where even now it could not keep from falling:
One of the green things under me was a man

who constantly spoke against me as I fell.
Part of my joy was knowing I turned him white
and covered him up until he spoke no more.
Afterwards the world was quiet, so I quit.
Not one thing looked alone or foolish; the place
felt safer, so I lay back and was happy.

# A Canticle of the Stars

I wanted to walk outside and praise the stars
for lending me lights to look by in the dark.
I wanted to look at them and name their names

like names of angels flocking among the saints
to lift the saints up into the holy fire
where they could look like angels with their own eyes.

I wanted to walk upright in the real world
before the light took over and I was light
or the light's kinsman in the skin. I wanted

to walk awhile in the green place near the edge
where sweeter things than I was took up the light
into their kindly fingers and it was light

where they were. Before the light was all there was
I wanted to walk around in the one world
once and for all, like other walking creatures

that made their way, taking up room in the dark,
striking the dark at both ends till they broke through
into the deep green space beside the waters

where dreamless beasts go quietly one by one
from light to shadow, nudging the dark aside
with their sweet faces. What could I do but look

and wipe my eyes? More gladness than I could stand
was all around me and it was their doing
or so I kept on thinking back in my mind

until they looked to find me and there I was,
preparing to dance my dance in so much light
I might have ascended in a beam of it

the way the saints did after they drank their fill
from Father Francis's cup of life and looked
tranquilly at the root of that golden tree

to see the angels flying into Christ's mind
while Christ was rapt in thinking about the sun
and how it writhes in fire for the likes of us.

## Saint Ambrose and the Bees

Asleep in his crib one warm summer morning
the young Saint Ambrose experienced bees
issuing from his mouth in a great swarm.
The nursemaid, probably a local heathen,
hurried off to summon the baby's parents,

who arrived in time to witness this wonder,
and his father was heard to prophesy,
as the bees disappeared into the sun,
that this child would achieve pre-eminence
in the Law or the Ministry or the Arts,

as had been marvelously intimated
by the magical visit of these bees.
Everyone agreed and rejoiced and prayed,
especially the Saint's elder sister,
Marcellina, who was a pious virgin.

This took place about the year 335,
when Constantine the Great was Emperor
and the Vandals still dwelt on the Danube
and the grandmother of Attila the Hun
was herself an infant, somewhere in Asia.

## The Saint and the Lady

The holy Serenus was a gardener
who used to love to caress his eggplants
and plump zucchini with a prayer like this
to God the Father: Lord of rind and seed,
think on Thy son, Serenus, in his need.

There was a tree that overarched his garden
and on it a sign that read: NO WOMEN—
HERMIT. But one day a lady wandered through
on her way home (after her lover went
his own way home through the bushes) and espied

Serenus gazing up at her from his hoe,
saying in his thin, brittle voice: Woman,
for shame. It is not meet for you to be here.
My garden is a holy place for God
and me, and womankind should not be found here.

Quite angry, she ran off and told her husband,
who was a fat and lethal governor,
so the blameless Serenus was dragged away
to have his head cut off by some soldiers.
He was styled a martyr on account of this.

## Kennedy

One late afternoon I hitched from Galway down to Kinvara on the edge of the Burren, one of those long midsummer days when the sun labors at last out of all-day rain and sets very late in the evening. In dark pubs all up and down the street, the townsmen hunched to their pints, silent and tentative as monks at supper. Thinking to take my daily Guinness, I stopped, and Kennedy was there, his picture on the mantel behind the bar.

A black-headed citizen half in his cups sidled over and smiled. Ah Kennedy Kennedy, a lovely man, he said and bought me a Guinness. Ah yes, a lovely man, I said, and thank you very much. Yes Kennedy, and they slaughtered him in his youth the filthy communists, he said, and will you want another. Yes, slaughtered him in his youth, I said and thanked him very much.

All night till closing time we drank to Kennedy and cursed the communists—all night, pint after pint of sour black lovely stout. And when it came Time, I and my skin and the soul inside my skin, all sour and lovely, strode where the sun still washed the evening, and the fields lay roundabout, and Kinvara slept in the sunlight, and Holy Ireland, all all asleep, while the grand brave light of day held darkness back like the whole Atlantic.

## Daffodils

It wasn't the daffodils so much
as the idea of them that got
me. I was wandering by in my
own lonely manner like a cloud in the sky
feeling ugly and grim when out
of nowhere up blossomed a clutch

of yellow daffodils by the curb.
Bright things they were, good and sweet,
and I knew I liked them better than
music or money or my girl's friendly skin
the way they stood there by the street
nicer and newer and simpler

by far than anything I had seen
all morning. Oh it was fine
to know them! I said, You daffodils
put me in mind of the clean white windowsills
of a kitchen when I was nine
one April Saturday in 19

52—my grandmother's kitchen,
her fingers dangling with dough,
the odor of pie in the oven,
the windows white as the windows of Heaven,
as if the air were bright with snow,
and someone outside them, watching.

## *In Praise of It*

To have a body is to learn to grieve.
Being alive means going it alone.
Of all the Ways, one is the holy one;
another leads to love and making love,
which I prefer, having made love to you
all morning and most of this afternoon,
coming to terms with much of the Unknown
we never knew was there. You made me do
it, and I liked it, and I said I did,
and I'd be glad to say it once again
in front of all these people. Furthermore,
I don't want to win souls or relieve pain.
If someone asks me what I do this for,
all I can say is, When you're good, you're good.

# Nineteenth of April
*Remembering Concord Bridge Two Hundred Years After*


1

I wanted to begin, so I began
by opening some windows and a door.
Next thing I did I brought one breath of air
straight down inside me. After that was done
I stuck my face outside to find the sun
because I wanted light to go with air,
and it was good light from the local star,
so I was glad to have it. Once a man
like me draws light around his bones, I thought,
it isn't long before the right things happen.
All that I did was make the windows open
because they bothered me when they were shut.
As for the door, I guess I'll go on out
after a little, if I feel like it.

2

I stood and looked and tried to think and thought
about the way the birds slid through the sky
down to the place I stood in, stupidly,
beside myself, stiff with confusion, fit
to die. I'd make a good case for the State
Patrol, I am my own worst enemy,
I said, They ought to come and get me, tie
me up, stick me away someplace to sit
and keep from trouble is what they should do.
Nubile the girls came squirming in their skins
among the breezes where the blackbirds flew.
One of them raised her arms so that the bones
beneath her little breasts were standing through.
The way she did that stung me in my brains.

3

The feckless gunman on the radio
bungled the stick-up and got shot and died.
I'd like to find out why a man can go
to such extremes to make his body dead.
You might say I'm a stickler for the truth
that lurks inside the baffling human breast
and shoves nice Mister Average off to death
some early morning in the Middle West.
Figure it out. One bad night in a dream
a bunch of women in a pick-up truck
pull up beside him with a jug of Beam.
The tall one with the tits says Like to fuck?
With that they take off down the Interstate.
Next day his guts get wiped up off the street.

4

Listen, the thing I had to say was this:
I said I'd write it down in a love-poem
for you this afternoon when you went home,
so here the sweet thing is: I'd like to kiss
each of the little hairs that make that stripe
that runs down from your navel to your crotch.
I don't think this is asking all that much.
I hope you won't think I'm the twisted type
that wants to put his face in a girl's hole
and rub his nose around among her cheeks.
I'm really a nice old man with a clean soul
from a family with a history of heart-attacks.
I cry at night. I fart. I've got this mole.
I'd really like to just go out for walks.

5

When I got through, I felt so good I said
Whenever a man like me gets good and ready
to get the word from what it is he is,
you'd tend to think that almost anybody
would take the fastest road out of the man's way.
Nineteenth of April. Buds are busting loose.
Can you believe it? Gunfire and bloodshed.
Don't shoot unless shot at, the Captain said,
in April, when the girls are full of juice
even in Massachusetts. What a day
to ruin your workshirt with a bullet-hole
or put a plug in some poor Sassenach
who had a favorite whore in Liverpool
who wasn't sorry when he wasn't back.